Where Hast Thou Thy Poets Gone?

Written By:
Abram Hollows

Illustrations By:
Lovanna Belle Amé

Mac Publishings—Fair Grove, MO
ISBN: 979-8-218-20870-7
Library of Congress Control Number: 2023909222
Title: *Where Hast Thou Thy Poets Gone?*
Author: Abram Hollows
Digital distribution | 2023
Paperback | 2023

Dedication

To my loving family who inspired me-
To the friends who challenged me-
To the sweetest memories of which I am fond
To the times of growing pains and past mistakes disdained-
To all of these and more - because of them I write once again.

A collection of poems written from 2017-2021

Where Hast Thou Thy Poets Gone?

Where hast thou thy poets gone?
There used to be so many
Have they taken Frost's road—
Or have they merely gone to and fro?

Since, they write in stanza bittersweet,
We hear their language never told,
Never hear timeless ends of stories old.
Were Emily's words, for the present, too petite?

Is life a stage? Does Death wear masks?
We fear change—
We feel pain—
But do we see the immortal human story?

Long gone have our poets been,
Their forgotten language now dead
Their stories forever unread
Are our greatest sin-

Where have thou thy poets gone?
There used to be so many

The Silhouette Girl

In the twilight I wander
Down the lively mountains
to the sleepy valley
There, I think
There, I dream
Dwelling on times of joy
The trees give way to dark, yet the sky glows orange
Like looking through curved glass
The valley bevels in the air

Then I see her dancing among other shadows—
As if she is one with the landscape
Though I know not what kind eyes she has—
No facial features show
All I know is the image of her form
And that is
Beauty.
She is one with the land and sky
Though all is seen in shadow
Her dance harmonizes with the valley

I watch and wonder what it would be like to dance
If my feet could carry this weathered man—
Oh, how I would fly!
But, alas, entranced by nature's true beauty
Though a picture is worth a thousand words,
This scene's brevity surpasses spoken language.

Only between night and day was I able to see this truth,
When shadow blurs all that I thought was real
Twilight takes me to the place

Where God and man were once united,
When heaven touches earth in its realest form
For a short time, we are in-between two phases—
Night and Day
And as the land and sky go dark,
The Silhouette Girl blends into the nightly shadows
Then the moon shines,
And all is no more

A Poet's Word

O poets, lend me your thoughts!
Conceive in your mind words like dreams,
Where young lovers soar,
Where Death may lurk
Speak, though truth is brutal,
Hacking through hearts like an ax against the grain
Pieces gliding across space and time

O poets, lend me your words,
That I may speak with the angels above
Or with the tongues of snakes
The truth that tastes like honey
Burns like fire rising in your throat.

O poets, lend me your strength -
That same strength you use to lift the iron pen from its paper
With that pen you write the truths we wish not to hear
For the word both binds us and
Calls us to action,
But we cover our ears

O poets, lend me your courage!
The day comes when I must lay my head to rest
I will let go of my work and pass it on
I shall go where no word or truth can follow
That, my friends will be the hardest to swallow
When we say goodbye -
That's when our own truth shall die

Dream Once Sought

Tonight, I end a fantasy -
Or was it a reality?
I lay down by calm waters
Anxiety rolls off my shoulders like a a rain-soaked cloak falling to the
ground
Closing my eyes for the first time in a long time,
The weight is gone,
The struggle no more
It's funny how a habit in your life fades over time
I know I'm falling asleep, but I've never felt more awake

This isn't me losing hope
Rather, I'm gaining my life back
Expectation is my enemy no more
I have finally given up the fight
I lay my weapons down beside me
No more attacks.
I have not given up the war, just this battle
I'm surrendering this battle
To win the war

I knew this was coming
Like an addict I kept returning to my drug
All is over now…
And when these words grow old-
I will have forgotten all
When these words grow old-
So will this night

I feel… Nothing.
No pain.

No regret.
Nothing.
I wish I felt something-
Then would I be considered human?
For now, I have given up
And though more battles will be fought
This ends a dream I once sought

Beholder's Fixation

A stolen glance or by happenstance,
Destiny, fate, coincidence
Or sheer dumb luck
Words spoken to describe our happy chance.
How does one conceive the price of art?
Who dons beauty and makes it so?
It be not but the mind's own Matrix,
Whose words divulge thy train of thought.

Betwixt the mind and flesh lies the soul of man
While brains are easily measured by education,
And brute strength by weight,
The spirit who can calculate?
Here lies the root cause of deep grief and abounding joy.

The spirit is a tender muscle not easily exercised,
If ignored, devastation oppresses the mortal body.
For deep within that fragile vessel lies one's aptitude,
Potential that some may never attain

Some say the broken shards of one soul can be found within another
If so, then how can such hearts be so easily turned?
Though thought of flesh satisfies briefly,
And the taste of wine dulls the mind for a moment
It is the Beholder's Fixation that will last
The driving force of the very soul
For the soul beats like a drum
Playing out our heart's pulse.

Obsession leads to mal content,

Corrupting the soul
But true beauty can save
For within the soul lies Grief, Sadness, Despair
Alongside Love, Peace, and Joy

So, a stolen glance or by happenstance,
Destiny, fate, coincidence
Or sheer dumb luck,
Can extinguished the flame within the soul, leave one awestruck.

Lady of the Night

Ding! Dong!
The clock strikes twelve
The party is livelier than ever
Champagne, the devil's choice tonight
A drunken slur, the throng wanders
No man understands the danger lurking
But there she walks-
Temptation's delight
No man's eye can turn away from such array

You are quick to judge
Beware - devils hide-
In more than curves or lips
There she walks
The Lady of the Night.

Dressed in scarlet red-
The unknown fear, the unknown dread
Her stride carries her to the far-left table.
"Anything to drink tonight, madam?"
"Champagne," is all she answers

Champagne, the devil's choice.
"No charge madam; compliments from the man over there."
She detects a tall, dark man hidden by a shadow
His suit is black and clean, his features all but hidden
"Tell him I wish to pay myself. Thank him, please."
She sips her wine, watching

The man seems to nod, disappearing into the shadows
A foreboding chill runs up the Lady's spine

She glances to and fro-
Across the room
All are oblivious to the scene,
Each man and woman concerned only with their free spirits

A small but firm voice pierces the Lady's train of thought
"May I sit with you?"
The dark man has appeared from behind
Scream no, say go. Say no. Run.
"Sure," her voice trembles
The man seems to smile but
Remains in the shadows

He sits; she folds her hands.
He whispers, "Are you afraid?"
Looking at him with a solemn composure
"Yes."
"You should be," the man says "Everyone is in merriment."

"And yet," he continues, "Not you."
She looks down, wordless
"That would make you wiser – stronger - wouldn't you say?"
She sits, motionless.

The man stands up, "You think you can win. You think you can
withstand my temptations?"
He bends down to whisper into her ear. "They all fall. Just you wait-
Soon you will join them."
"You're wrong," Her voice cracks.
Now she sees his white teeth grinning
"The longer you stay the weaker you become.
Enjoy yourself madam."
Then he is gone into the night

She rises from the table, her glass falling
A bubbly river spilling onto the floor
As she finds herself alone
All party-goers consumed by the night

In a moment, she too will dissolve,
Joining the fading mist of intoxicated air

A man in a white suit materializes

"Your car, madam, awaits."
She strides to the gate
Her rescue, her escape
As she glances back, she sees him on the balcony
The dark man starring
Like he has never seen anyone want to leave
She enters car and departs
And in the rearview mirror she sees him grin no more

Wisdoms Lore

If we truly understood wisdom's lore
O how the heart of man would soar!
The depths of knowledge might we reach—
If only Time's tentacles did not lives leech

For Wisdom is Time's old friend
Neither of which can no man offend
If only we could touch their limit
But that is beyond my wit

O how I have knocked on the doors of time,
Listened to the sounds of love's sweet rhyme!
But alas! Wisdom could not be found
Man's true mind is like dust of the ground

Lore of Anger

Thou hast not seen a tempest, Anger, such as thee
From olden rhyme telling of ageing time
Since then the world hast felt thy raging word

From wisping bundles in fields of country yore
To tales of valiant men from fabled lore
Your gales like eagles soar

While legends speak of your grace,
Only cruelty will grace your tomb's face.
Remembering your rotting corpse in this place

So, vomit your words of fury upon me
When you have spent your last dime, enshrined your last crime
They surely will think your practice of wrath absurd

Sunrise

Nature unfolds through many appearances,
Shining eyes peeking over clouds of yonder sky
We see the waltz in every shadow gliding along the earth below.
As if God the azure canvas too confining for His untamed beauty.
A paint brush He holds, flinging drops of gold splashing on upward
sky
The love He planted in nature
Sprouts tendrils in my heart
O how wealthy am I to awaken daily to this gallery!

Sunset

The clouds pile up like pillows in the west
Shadows stretching a cot between earth and sky,
The dual expanses of young lovers embracing in the night
The blaze of orange and red fade in the hearth
A sense of calmness descends on the land
A cool sheet settling,
As stars poke out their nodding heads
The fresh whisper of night's "sleep tight" sooths our brow

Haiku 1
If we run away
Far, far, far away from here
Then we have no fear.

Haiku 2
What love I had known
From the rays of the huge sun
Father of the Jews.

Haiku 3
Here we meet again
At the place where I can't stand
Forgive me I pray.

Haiku 4
High school love is a-
Joke. It comes and it will go
So why do we try?

Wind's Wisdom

While a caressing breeze brings sweet relief on a scorching day,
A great gust topples any haphazard structure
Be careful what you wish for, my friend
For what seems good the moment
Can ruin you in the end
Those who float with the wind
Either bring life or destruction
Whatever they touch they affect

The Love You're Looking For

Your quest for love will get you none,
But your walk through life may get you some
I hate goodbyes but I say them anyway
You hold my hand and beg me to stay.

That look in my eye you loathe,
Because my glance shows my heart unclothed
My heart races at the thought of leaving
Of all the glory of the journey's receiving

With a gentle kiss I lay to end
All the questions that could amend
And so, I walk out that door
I wasn't the love you were looking for

Sands of Time

Chasing away the sands of time
Doesn't that sound like a lovely rhyme?
Her body is that of an hourglass,
Her waist so thin not even sand can pass
This, alas, cannot last

Chasing away the sands of time
People would give a pretty dime
For any old good time
They drink to be merry
As their eyes grow weary
Chasing away the sands of time

No matter where time comes from—
It will always leave
No matter what you try,
No matter how you plead
Wasting time is such a crime
Chasing away the sands of time

Return Me to the Mountain

Return me to the mountain of my youth.
Where steady streams roared with unheard laughter-
And the trees whispered among themselves in autumn breeze
Oh, the sounds of the mountains still ring in my head!

There is a place where sky and earth touch-
Where clouds fall-
I find my rest. And there I stay-
Deep in thought-
Where I pray.

This place is like no other;
The sun rests on the mountain's gentle crest
And in evening glow the clouds dance like shadows
The mountain can touch heaven
When I cannot
The mountain speaks of peace
When I am at war with the world
The rock face is wise

At last, I must leave
I pray, someday, that I will return-
Return to that mountain I once knew

Hast, Thou Forgotten Me

Hast thou forgotten me?
What love shared just a few days past
Hast thou forgotten me?
I held you close and tight
Hast thou forgotten me?
My fingers ran through your hair
Hast thou forgotten me?
Now you play with the boy next door
Hast thou forgotten me?
Your tail used to wag when I petted you
Hast thou forgotten me?
Goodbye my German friend -
Until we meet again

Kindness' Cake

One cup of kindness may save a cake
Put it in life's oven and watch it bake
See it rise and behold what you make
Don't forget kindness a lifelong mistake
Share a piece with a neighbor, give and take

Call to Action

Where can one find the answers?
Does not knowledge come from within ourselves?
We think about problems and solutions,
But so
few
act.

White Line

The blinding white line appeared like in a dream
As the snow fell from heaven's doorstep
Small pockets of steam formed around my breath
Like clouds on a moonbeam

The line stretched across the road
As if beckoning me into the nearby field
A cape of snow now shrouded the landscape
Only the ringing of silence in my ear

I walked gently beside the white line,
Carful not to disturb the night around me
My footprints are like canyons
The only blemishes on a perfect plain of powder

All seems empty until the line's end
Where rises a skeleton bush with one weathered rose.
The heartbreaking red flower pierces my soul
This is life ten thousand-fold

Truly Alone

I whisper. No one hears.
I speak. No one replies.
I scream at the top of my lungs. Silence.

I'm alone. Truly alone.
Inside this fortress of stone.
I have retreated within the walls of my heart.
Into the sanctuary of my soul.
Cold. It's cold.

Maybe this is just a dream. No, a nightmare.
I can't wake up. I won't wake up.
The isolation of one man seems meaningless.
Only when you are the one isolated will you wake up.
Only when you're alone will you know.
Truly void.

Walk in the woods and a tree falls.
Does it make a sound even if no one's around?
I don't know - ask the tree.

I'm alone. Truly alone.
If I screamed who would come?
No one…

But here I am.
I make a noise, even if you can't hear it.
I still do good, even if you can't see it.
I still love, even if you can't feel it.
I'm alone.
In my integrity
Truly alone.

Binding Creed

There is an unspoken word -
A bond that we live by
We walk through the streets with our heads held
High
But how have the mighty fallen?
They are bound by an unspoken word,
A creed
That the honorable and the proud must follow
If they are to keep their name's weight in gold

We all know the tragedy of the proud
Pride
By this word good men will quarrel
By this word they shall fight
For their separate creeds
Though both are honorable, one cannot exist-
While the other lives on

Why you ask?
Because of pride – one's right, one's wrong
So, the earth will consume their blood
Until one yields. Until one breaks. Until one's death.
Peace
Can be no more
This my friends is our binding creed
Until one attains a more noble deed

Selfish Creed

People wish to live true love's fairytale.
While they race too quickly through life's dance
False love drives them to insanity
They whip up a windstorm with sloppy Romance
Their hearts wandering led astray
Our forefathers are put to shame
Hear me brothers: Wisdom has retreated
Really who is to blame?
If it had not been for our doing
Would our sins have come into the light?
We have seen too much overreaching pursuit
Will humans ever know true love's full height?
This shall forever be a decree -
All men are filled with selfish greed

What You Taught Me

Those woods we used to know,
Where autumn leaves fall,
Time stands still
In this moment of memory
Wisdom shows through your work
Down here on earth

You taught us many things -
How kindness returns in kindness
How hope can carry a broken heart
How love can save us all

The things you showed us
The things you still teach us
The things that you taught me
The things I carry

You taught me how to say goodbye
When all I wanted was to hold you-
You taught me to let go
But the last thing you taught me-
Is how to let love grow

Unearthed Hearts

Unearthed hearts we see in true form
If I sought to discover what lies beneath the surface,
If I look, would you unpeel the calluses from your worn heart?
What then do I find?
We conceal our intentions behind sarcasm and lies

Here I stand in wonder
       Searching for thoughts I used to ponder
           Once this heart did love
But at last, that love would come to pass.

For what is true among feelings?
Surely not evidence - couldn't be
No courtroom case would accept such circumstantial proof
And yet we try-
       To use our hearts to pry

For if you ever loved, you do not now
I see through the facades
       I see through the lies
Unearthed hearts we see in true form
Not of love but vanity -
Our truest sanity

The Fool of Books

Education, my friends, has come a long away
We know the things our fathers didn't
Progress.
That's what man says as he studies science and nature
Man looks within his mind for the answers now
Rather than to a natural occurrence
Or to some bedtime story he has heard
Gone are the days of God's punishing people,
For man is now his own "god"

Man sits in his studies, his libraries, his labs
He thinks and ponder on his theories-
That can never be proven
He tries to reason
He tries to create his own truths
But truth is set in stone
Perceptions.
That is what man suggests when he wishes
Not to argue
"That is your perspective on life," he says,
As if perception is an answer at all

So, man studies.
He writes it down in books
Which he passes down to the young.
He says, "Read this for this is truth."

Life goes on
The books are read
The young teach the younger undeveloped minds
The new man studies just like his father

Yet education my friends has died
Education has become too advanced for common sense
The new man only trusts his mind

And so, what he once thought was truth now crumples before him
For he is in the generation of the end; no books can save him now
Man is his own "god" and therefore must find his own salvation
But man has no salvation
For man has no truth
He is the fool of books

Untitled Love

I have loved you from the start
You waltzed away with my heart
Remember us when we were young
Vibrant and free?
We always talked like we we're the only ones-
In the world.
It never seemed to rain
Now all I spy are clouds

Heart Sings

O how my heart sings to you O God!
I lift my hands to heaven
I kneel in your awesome presence
I rest on your foundation
You are the rock of my life
I will love you forevermore.

A Day to Come

I knew this day would come
We all knew
I just never thought it would come so soon
You think for a moment-
That life is everlasting
You think for a moment-
That these seconds are eternal
Imagine

Fabric of Time

This sliver of eternity,
A tear in the fabric of time
This exact moment of existence
None have ever yet seen this second.

Here we are… living it
We never know
What may arrive
Next

The Lucky Ones

They say love is for the lucky ones
Two lovers sat on a steamboat watching the night
The river carrying them gently downstream
The air was clear and the moon full
As they drifted under the sky,
The air grew colder

She shivered a little-
So he drew her close in a warm hug
She smiled and leaned on his shoulder.
No words were spoken-
And yet all was understood

Love needs no words to describe itself
Only through action does one's love show
They say love is for the lucky ones
He never believed in such a love-
Until the day he met her
Only by chance did these two souls cross

He was wild and free-
She was kind and sweet
From across the room, he saw her
Deep down he knew-
He would never be the same

She noticed him across the room
Her smilewarm as the glow of the lamp

The smile drew him to her-
And soon they were together.
It's funny they say love is for the lucky ones
As time passed, they got to know each other

Ice cream in July-
Coffee in September-
Hot chocolate in January-
Man, how time flew!
As the years went on, they knew-
A family would grow from these two
Indeed, four more joined them
Two girls-
Two boys.
And they say love is for the lucky ones

Still time went on
The children grew and moved away
They too were lucky and found love
They too would live in this love

And on that night as the water pushed them along-
She said, "Do you love me?"
He replied "Yes, I love you more now than when I first saw you."
"I love you more too."
The steamboat sailed through the night
And they say love is for the lucky ones

Through The Window

Their it came to me-
A story unfolding in my misty mind-

In the '50s diner he sat all tall but brooding,
A man whose work had left him weary
His gentle eyes peered longingly out the window
Though the dance floor was all but full,
The young throng flowing with merry couples

The man, however, sat on the bar stool
The window seemed to have captured his focus-
As he captured mine
I thought it strange-
For him to be here when his mind was of leaving.
I sipped my drink
Watching
Waiting

But the man barely breathed
Peering out that window
When I'd drained my drink, I joined the dance
Through music and laughter, I came alive
And I met the fairest one.

She wore a red shirt and blue jeans-
Flower in her hair and a soul-melting smile
A moment goes by as she enters the dance floor
I hold out my hand and
We danced into darkness

She was, herself, a drifter in the night

Never growing roots,
Hearing her story,
I thought suddenly
Of the man peering out the window.

But at last, he sat there no more
The music ended and I said my goodbye
As I walked out the door there the man caught my eye
He walked up to the girl in red and-
From there they danced
Though the music was dying down
They didn't seem to mind

They were like two flames meeting
As he danced, I could see-
Liveliness becoming free
And her, breathing anew

The door closed behind me.
In the snow I smiled-
As I peered
Through the window.

Love Beyond the Grave

Till death do us part -
That's how it all starts

In a moment, an entire world can change-
A blink of an eye-
A spoken word-
A touch-
In one single moment, my existence transfigures

It's not just you-
It's not just me-
It's us forever

For that moment everything is perfect
There is no fighting-
No screaming kids in the backseat of your car
No bills to pay
No angry words to say
Just us.
Framed in time.

Life is made of moments like this
We wish they will last.
But in the end, the memory is all we have

In the finale moment
When the fullness of time has come
When a breath takes an eternity
And you cling to their hand
Promising to never let go
You beg to go with them

But the road they travel
Is one-lane highway
Here is where we part ways

I pray you take my heart to save
For all the love beyond the grave

My Mind. My Prison.

My mind - my prison.
Only those who dare test limits of existence explore the mind
More than a mere organic shape
More than a mere tissue protected by bone
Man's best tool.

The mind can change the world
And make inmates out of man
Thoughts
Actions
Words
Originate in the mind.
Driven by motive
While inner desires lurk within the cobwebs
Connecting cogs in the machinery of mass destruction
A perpetually ticking time bomb

The mind is power
A secret weapon of the dangerous
Monsters who take advantage of the weak minds
String the mind along; play it like a violin
Although the mind is the weight of gravity

Oh, where is the birthplace of evil?
Is it not in the mind?
Where do our obsessions come from?
If not from the mind, then where?

This is the curse of the intellectuals,
Those who are imprisoned by
Driven us to insanity
Since the pursuit of knowledge exhausts

We try to find perfection-
But we come up short
We try to fill the void in our soul -
Oh, never-ending void!

Man develops his own philosophies
What's right and what's wrong?
Is man the judge of right and wrong?
We doom our world
The mind is power
The mind is controlling
The mind is a bank for knowledge,
A cold vault
Emotionless musings
Only logic.
Loveless ponderings
-Only cold facts-

Heroes of Old

My heart is full of woe -
O how the generation has fallen,
The legends are now nothing more than myths.

Where are the men so desperately needed?
Where are the women of virtue and value?
Though wisdom is forgotten, it is never lost

We seek, in a society of chaos, a hero to stand
One who will take the risk and be the man
But alas, still we seek this hero's name
Lost

My Solemn Prayer

I long to know your heart
The desperate thirst within my soul is unbearable
Your love never fails
I call out for that love,
The love by which you saved my soul
The fire you kindled in my heart long ago-
Still burns to this day.
Though the road has been wearying,
When I sleep exhausted
I dream of you

I cry out to you
My hour of need has lasts for eternity
My enemies threaten the gates
I know I don't fight alone for you are with me
The sword you raise for my cause is mighty
I cry out to you

Forgive me, Lord for I have stumbled
I have fallen, though you have never let me go
By grace I was freed
I would bleed to save my fellow friends
But their salvation is beyond my reach
It is their choice alone
Forgive me, Lord
Thank you for loving me
Now I sin no more

Jungle of my Mind

When I dream, my dream consumes my mind
Shadows dance on the walls of my brain
My fears brought to light
My shame uncovered,
I walk this grassy path.
Leading into the wilderness

Here I walk between reality and fantasy
Here I wander the jungles of my mind
The mighty lion steps forth,
The king claiming his realm.
At his roar, the jungle grows silent

The animals respect this great king
Wolves, elephants, tigers, panthers
Beasts of the wilderness respect this monarch
Bowing at his blast

When the apes arc from branch to branch
When exotic birds glide above the trees
When rhinos rumble across the fields
When bears embark on the hunt
When wolves howl at the moon -
This is when my heart goes wild

In the jungle of my mind, I can see the vivid image -
A glimpse of once was -
Before
Man tore the jungle down
Manufactured a tangle of concrete and metal
Before the cages and imitations of wilderness

This image I see -
The lion looking over his vast kingdom of green
Jungle and plains
Watering holes and oases
Paradise

Then I wake.
The king and his kingdom is are concrete
A statue
Gracing the gates leading to this man-made jungle
When I wake
All is gone

Stairsteps to Heaven.

Looking to heaven, I gaze into the unending cosmic glow, where clouds and moon meet
Stars twinkle as clouds hang suspended in midair
As if a stairstep to heaven begins and ends right about there

A beauty untold can be seen in the heavens if anyone bothered to look
With the tilting of the head, one perceives the majesty and beauty above
Instead, we are wrapped up in our dull world
Constantly looking down at the dirt and the soil
Like this we are forced to work the land, to harvest, to toil

While some look up and dream of stairsteps to heaven-
Others look down and only see clay
While one thinks of new things
The others walk the daily mundane, ever trudging the same

I observe the dreamer's habits
While some are stuck on earth, others fly
One man toils the other imagines
But even the dreamer resigns, works to survive
And so, dies another dream upon the stairsteps to heaven

Remind Me

If I forget, help me remember
Help me remember the good times
When we used to laugh, sing, and dream
Remind me of that day-
That hour when all was right

When Love Conquers All

What has happened to the human mind?
Have we forgotten our rudimentary basics?
The very ideas that make us human-
Love, compassion, honesty, faith, hope

Yes, we have forgotten my dear friends
Instead of love there is hate between us
O how we have become divided!
Man has drawn a line where there was none
Just as they did in the days of creation

The ideals of man were born into his children
Greed, hate, lust, shame, self-indulgence, laziness-
Pride
We are divided, and divided we fall
Divided then we cannot win
Sometimes I wish intelligence never existed
The simple are lucky
They shed world's worries and woes
If pride is the root of our evil-
And pride is born with in our own mind-
Our own intelligence-
Why do we seek knowledge?

Love is unsolvable
The intelligent bypass love
Love doesn't result from an equation
Though love is the solution to all our problems
For this reason, the intelligent cannot understand love

Truly loving one another would sow a peaceful world

Devoid of problem-solving
Instead, our quest is to grasp knowledge
Produces affection-quenching intelligence

If love conquered all
Intelligence would dissolve like a vapor in the wind
Simple people with simple love
A solution too complex for a society of the brain
Pride-
Hate-
For this reason they cannot embrace love
And so, love is their downfall
Because love conquers all

The Eclipse

For a short moment all seems different
The space and time of our reality is revealed in the sky
For the first time in ages the moon and the sun meet
They face each other only for a moment-
A moment lasting for eternity

She wanders in the night sky
Each night a lantern for travelers.
The waves bow as she wades in the heavens
The stars twinkle en masse as she passes by
Preforming their duty as her entourage

His blaze lights the day sky
Men work under command of his shining rays
Even as he rules the earth from afar
Each day he ascends his throne.
Without him all life fails

The moon pledged to guiding travelers to dawn
Leaves no time for her dearest one
Searching the globe for the sovereign of the golden ray
Duties of the night and day
Conflictions
Forever longing but never graced in love's presence

The sun is restrained from his long-lost love
For the day demands so much
Life depends on him, and he must provide
He rules from his lonely throne in the heavens
Loyally obligated to care of his people

But on this day, fortuitously a meeting occurs
Though approaching night darkens his world, he waits eagerly
For in the darkness, a light shall shine
From out darkness, a familiar light glows

She advances toward his throne
Since ages past has she not stood here
Until this day she walked his way
In this moment two are one
For a moment they embrace

Only tears of joy flood his eyes-
And hers pool too
For in this moment, they are together
She hasn't changed in his eyes;
Her beauty is beyond compare

The world stops in wonder
People and animals watch with awe
Why have night and day collided on this comic date?

The sun knows the earth can't last without him;
The moon understands that their time is short
She begins to leave.
They hold on to each other, lingering as they drift apart
When she's gone his world is void

Yet she carries his light with her wherever she goes
Though the sun misses her, this job he chose
But when they meet oh how they will be glad!

And so, the earth and I think and ponder
Of the eclipse and the moon that wanders

Lost

My love for thee has never failed - until now
This moment just out of reach
Like a leaf blowing in the wind

I stop and listen to the rumble of the beach,
The roaring waves which echo in my brain
I know I never really understood love
Because it echoes in my brain

We over think and never truly feel
I said, "I love you" and you said, "But how can we love?"
You were right of course - two tortured artists we were
Through selfish pride we held hands into the future

As time goes on, we grow apart
I never knew separation could feel this frigid
I have found another after all these years,
But let's be honest - I never could love her

As I look into her eyes, seeing the reflection of you
Her eyes lead me to your soul and free spirit
If they really did then maybe I would be satisfied
But, alas, I am unquenched

I pray she never finds out the truth
I have always loved you
Though my heart has never found the words to say
It is like chasing that leaf, forever out of reach

Angel of the Night

The angel of the night whispers softly,
Quietly among the woodland roads
Small sighs dance in the night's wind
While the stars shimmer in the blackened sky

O how the eve's green has turned to red, orange, and yellow
And then to tomb black
The soft gasp of gentle leaves hitting the autumn ground
The only sound among the woodland roads

The moon gazes towards the earthly scene,
Watching the peaceful landscape
From the heavens she descends
To the forgotten woodland road

As her foot touches the ground all around the earth lights up
The meadow radiates as if a hundred thousand fireflies were set loose
She stands on solid soil
Her mineral brown hair veiling her face
Her wings spread out with angelic grace

She takes in the tranquil landscape before going to work
In that moment all seems serene
The flames, however, reach to incinerate the heavens
The scorching blaze threatens hell
She slowly turns and faces the horror of the night

A maroon Chevy Malibu burns next to a broken fence piled beneath a tree
A man slumps over the wheel motionless,
Warm rush of blood spewing from his flushed lips
The woman in the passenger side lies on the dash,
Her skull cracked, her breathe slow

The angel of the night is the first to appear on the scene

No first responders. No witnesses. No firemen. No one.
Only the angel watches the woman in the car
Whose breath has grown faint
The man wakes, diagonal in distress

The angel watches from the outside
As the man comes to, realizing the horror of the night
He looks at the woman, whose breathe is barely there
He stumbles out of the car
Dragging the woman with him,
Laying her on the shoulder of the woodland road

Frantically he scans the lonely road.
Then races back to the car
The angel peers over the woman in wonder
As the man returns with phone in hand
Only to find the signal dead
Dead

The man cradles his lover in the night
He screams for help, unheeded,
By all but the angel of the night
She bends down, placing a hand on the man's shoulder

A warm rush passes over the man
And the woman wakes for just one moment
Just a smile
And a breath.
Her eyes close
It's quiet among the woodland roads

Tears drown the man's eyes.
Diamond drops fall upon the dead woman's face
In that moment all is dark
Until a new star is born in heaven tonight
The woman, guided by the angel
Upon that sorrowful and tragic night,
The woman now gazes down with delight

Her pain is no more
But her heart still aches for the man abandoned
If only he could see his world from above
Maybe he would know how to truly love
Quietly among the woodland roads

The Unknown Artist

As I stand admiring the painting on the wall, it occurs
A sort of thought-
An emotion, I guess
Is beauty truly in the eye of the beholder?
I ponder as I gaze into the simple scene
A tree painted beside a stone fence,
The sky ablaze with poppy and peony glow radiating from the sunset's
gaze

It's a painting, made from simple oils
It's canvas of simple origins
It had not occurred to me to wonder:
Who is the artist?
A name of no consequence appears-
Underneath the art is just one word:
"Unknown"

Unsatisfying
Does appreciation decline if the artist is a ghost?
The name of the piece leaves even more to be desired-
"My Silent Dream"
What is that supposed to mean?
I have too many questions, no answers

The colors flicker when the sun passes over the painting
Bringing a newness to the scene
The colors mash together to form a bluish scene,
Sort of dreamlike-
Maybe I was too quick to critique

I have seen a good many paintings in my day-

But none has ever inspired me like this one
For the first time I realized
I truly do not know art
Michelangelo painted immortal view
But this unknown artist molded a simple work-
Framing beauty masterfully
I judge the art too hastily when I know the artist,
Depending on if I like his or her previous works
But I had no idea who painted this painting
And the point is the unknown

So, one must look at this one piece
To see if the artist knows pain or beauty-
Happiness or sorrow
Evil or good
From this one piece I do know this-
That I truly do not love art.
I am only fooling myself

I do not truly understand the hours of labor
I did not slave under a lamp, hunched over a blank sheet
I didn't lift a finger to birth something beautiful
I just stand from a safe distance
Judging the new existence

I feel when I see the art.
I like or dislike a painting or a sculpture
Despite my ignorance of the artist's struggle
If I love the artist, then I love the art
If I love the art, then I love the artist
An infinity sign between the art and the artist

But how many have seen this exact painting?
Who was the art for?
For me?
For the artist?
I say both…
Is beauty really in the eye of the beholder?

I say the beholder can't fully comprehend the gravity of the creation
We point fingers and judge thoroughly
But our perspective is only our view
The sun sets behind me and the colors resume their original look
I take my last glance and continue through the gallery
Never before has a painting challenged me
To know that art is not only what I see

A Song Not Yet Heard

A song not yet heard from the lips of heaven,
Beauty veiled to the gaze of passion
The enchanting hour: the stroke of eleven
Is one to be draped in elegant fashion

Though none have yet conquered the ballroom floor
She waltzes among angels, flitting from wall to wall
From this moment I know she was born to soar
And I, most humble, to fall

Now I know she is more than diamonds or gold
And I wish I could call her mine
Though I believed every lie I was told
I will still love her till the end of time

Refine Wine

When I've had too much wine
The sun begins to shine
Ruby hues through the glass
Drink until we are gone, alas!

Reason or Heart

A man of science and reason-
Watches the sky during the change of season
His studies lead his wandering eye
Beyond the lunar eclipse and sky
Til a brightly lit star catches his gaze
His heart burning, he is utterly amazed
He never saw a celestial body such as this-
A beauty he nearly missed
Since he wishes to be with his star
Alas, he has been resigned to earth thus far

The Dying Dream

They say the dream will never die
That's not true.
All things pass-
The moment when you stop believing-
That's the moment the idea dies
The dream disappears

We try to keep the dream alive
For our children and children's children
The dream must survive
For freedom has a price
And patriots all know too well that bloody price

Gone are the days of noble men,
Of good over evil
Now we merely try to preserve what they died for
Out of respect, not eagerness
Oorah! They cry.
Oorah! they say as they die

For God and country-
Bleed
Let your blood run on this nation
Those who despise you
Those who call you heroes
Those who wish to join you
Those who spit in your face

The flag you raise they trample
The flag you bled for-
They burn

The freedom they take for granted
They will never understand

They say the dream will never die
The sacrifices were too great to forget
But the few who still remember-
Are old and gray
They say the dream will never die

Freedom

Freedom
The word is worth far more than what money can buy
It's what we live for,
Die for
Freedom - its price is blood
No one can steal it
No law
No words
No tyrants

When General Washington crossed the Delaware-
When the Gettysburg Address was spoken-
When all Amendment Rights were fought for-
That was freedom
When we all work for this American Dream-
We see liberty comes to light
When you sweat-
Bleed-
Bruise-
Through civil duty we pay the price of
Freedom.
How have we forgotten the sacrifice?
We march in our pretty parades
We drive down our paved roads
The everyday life leaves us absentminded
Freedom is so familiar that we have made it common
The work of our fathers have done
The battles they have won
Will all be in vain-
If we forget

But we won't
The song of freedom broadcasts
From Lady Liberty-
Echoing through the hills-
Skimming the mountains-
To the ocean's expansive bay
As long as I live, freedom will never be forgotten
To my children:
I pray you still fight for freedom every day
To America-
We will let freedom lead

Shoot for the Stars

I had a dream
A dream to shoot for the stars
Most people laughed; others sighed
But I had a dream

I went to work on my red rocket ship
Colored it red with a blue window
I showed it to my dad,
"Hey son, That ain't half bad,"

I had a dream
A dream to shoot for the stars.
Undeterred by people's scoffing
I had dream and nothing more
I met wonderful people along the way
Some friends came but most never stayed
I had a dream, a dream to shoot for the stars

People said that there is no road to the stars
No cars can drive that far, no planes, no busses
Only a rocket ship which was beyond me
Little did they know, I had a dream
And so, to work I went,
On my little rocket ship
Most people laughed; others sighed
"He will never reach the stars in that!"

Through the years they laughed
But I didn't mind
My place was among the stars
One day a girl passed by

While I was tinkering with my rocket
"What is that?" she asked
"It's my rocket ship," I replied
"Looks like a lot of work, do you need help?"

No one had ever offered such a grace
I handed her a wrench, and her fingers raced
We had a dream, a dream to shoot for the stars
Together we worked on my rocket
Day by day she would walk by
And stop to help
She saw most of my failures
And when I fell apart.

Among the laughers and scoffers, she was a kind face
A friend to boost me reach my destined place
The day came that my rocket was complete
Everyone came, though they tried to be discreet

They all came: the ones who mocked me,
The doubters, and the few believers
They all came to see me leave
I never really belonged to this world I thought
I saw her standing there with a smile that stalled my heart
If this world was more like her, maybe I would have stayed

But I had a dream, a dream to shoot for the stars
This was my moment
My time had come
That fateful hour felt so sweet yet so sour
Exploration and loss of the familiar

As the rockets burst into life, a reddish storm begins
A billowing noise grumbles through the air
People duck and hide
But she stands her ground and watches my little red rocket shoot for the
stars

There are no roads, no trains, no planes, nor even cars-
That could ever reach the stars
I looked down at everything I was leaving
Sad that I couldn't bring the best parts of this world

But I had a dream, a dream to shoot for the stars
It didn't matter the cost; it didn't matter how far
Now me and that girl are two worlds apart
But she knows her way, and she is smart

Now I'm among the stars where I knew I would be.
They said it would never happen to me
The worlds and stars up here outshine
The bare world below, on this mission all mine.

I had a dream, a dream to shoot for the stars
Now they don't seem quite so far

The King's Fool

Tonight, we end another fantasy
It wounds more than all other memory
Though I've been loves fool before
And I've felt the slamming door

In my mind I see it clearly
My dearest, I say sincerely
I wish you all the best -
Love and eternal rest

As a jester plays a fool for the king,
I let you strum my heart strings
But I have played as the biggest fool
For I have allowed you my heart to rule

You have trapped me in the lion's den
And exposed my greatest sin.
But, alas, you I cannot hate
For my mistress is my fate

This the hardest lesson I ever learned
Your sweet affection I never earned
I could not force love to bend
Now I know how it all will end

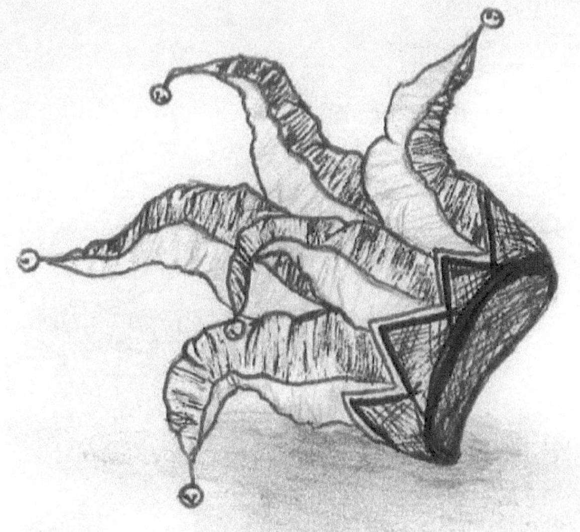

Love to Love Again

It may be fate that makes two lovers betrothed
By one's expression or by a single rose
Thus in her heart, she expresses such love
O how your love takes flight like a dove

But in mind you must keep -
Love may not risk the full leap
With time or miles, I do not know
If love will find thee on stage or show

For love's full rite takes more than your own heart
It requires understanding from the start
That love requires reciprocal hearts to align,
Two people's fates forever intertwined

O how a heart may betray
When one heart has nothing to say!
Expectations may linger un-met
And thus cause the heart to fret

For when double connection is not made
And only one heart love doth sway.
When only one loves with no love return.
O how an anger and sadness may burn.

If such passion in soul remains today,
I dare make a bold statement and say:
Love to love again
Do this until the road's end

Love with no return expectation,

Even in anguished proclamation
But do not spend all your willing self
For a heart that hides on its own shelf

Love is a treasure to behold,
A testament that has stood the test of old
For love is the greatest wealth on earth
Love guides us from the womb to the dirt

Fading Beauty

Looking at an old, faded polaroid I see how time washes away everything.
The once perfect and solid lines that separated colors and shapes now are blurred into a mush of smudged hues, leaving nothing but a distorted picture of the past.
I guess that's why life is digital now.
So we can remember clearly what we saw and what we said.
Sure, you can delete things and send their codes through the wide spectrum of cyberspace never to be seen again, but somehow those damned ones and zeros never really fade away.
At least a polaroid you can burn or tear to shreds.

But still, it's so hard to press the delete button.
Just a click and the present past will all be erased, gone from history, extinguished from existence.
The hardest things to do may just as well be the easiest things to do.
Like saying goodbye.
Goodbye.
It's not that hard to say.
It's natural.
Easy.
Then why so hard?

Sometimes I feel like I need to be in control of everything, because I can't even control myself.
I'm not good with emotions, but so I have mastered control over them instead.
Sometimes I see myself slipping and falling apart but never when anyone's around.
It's easier to suffer that way.

When eyes gaze down, feeling pity, feeling bad for you, or, worse
feeling nothing for you at all…
I'd rather just be alone.

They say Beauty doesn't last.
Ok, fine, but what if it did?
What if Beauty never really disappeared?
You see, some things do last. They, just fade in the process.
Like Beauty.
Look at the polaroid now versus when it was taken.
The lines and shapes blur together but the moment is still pure.
The memories frozen untainted by time's true pain –
The Fading Beauty.

The Trampled Rose

If you ever find a rose, you might as well leave it alone.
No matter its beauty you're love-stricken to the bone
The rose boasts thorns along its stem
And beauty is more than the surface of skin

I find myself angry at this stupid rose
For I picked it with gentle repose
It left a prick,
And it left me love sick
How could I have been such a fool?
Possessing a wild rose must violate the rules

But maybe I wish not to rule such a rose
Sometimes I wish time just froze
Sometimes I wish I didn't know what I know now
I could look back at you and smile somehow

What controls the rain, the sun, the clouds up above?
I know this cannot be controlled by love
Yet it is the driving force of the rose's growth
Forget man's laws or sacred oaths.

Whether it be storms or a sunny sky,
The rose finds a way to survive
With or without me
And without me it chooses to be

Still, the rose was trampled on
As I ventured upon its path alone
I couldn't leave such a beauty in dismay
So, I got my hands dirty that day

I tried to take the rose for my own
As if I had a right to roses thrown
The thorn pricked and drew blood dew
A lesson was taught and somehow I knew

If you ever find a rose, you might as well leave it alone
Because in the end you will only reap what you have sown

Adam's True Sin

What intruded on Adam's mind when he bit into the pulsing fruit?
Was it greed, lust of knowledge, or craving to God's one own equal?
For homo sapiens - wise, wise man - have always been credited with such insight.
Yet we play the part of the fool too often to ignore

Thus, might I wonder where life would be without such lustful greed,
If man could step down from his highest sin, pride of the noble steed?
Young hearts are often the victims to man's crooked deeds,
Vigorous and infamous inventions that sow the future's seeds.

If man holds power to create and destroy, why choose the latter?
If man shall create then build a world worth living in!
If resigned to destruction, finish off the earth like your enemy
Mother Earth has handed you the world; you wounded instead of worship

The fabric of our existence was entrusted to us
Yet man backed away from our divine duty,
And built a fake world of screens and broken dreams
The lie tended as truth, and the truth is left to the weeds

We mend a broken arm but fail at mending a broken soul
We talk with each other across the globe, but silent is our tongue with our neighbors
We can create and cure pandemics, but we cannot create true joy or cure depression
We treasure what we hoard, but we dismiss those we treasure

What intruded on Adam's mind when he bit into the pulsing fruit?
Was it greed, lust of knowledge, or craving to God's one own equal?

For homo sapiens - wise, wise man - have always been credited with such insight.
Yet we play the part of the fool too often to ignore

What weighs on man's true mind when he walks on the earth that never grew,
When greed has slain and taken hold of everything that was supposed to be made new?

The Journey

From the lively mountains to the ocean bay,
I, a hollowed man was called to sail away
Though dawn's true light had turned to solid night
My conviction stayed the same
I knew not what worlds awaited me on my fateful journey
But my heart was filled with excitement to reach such beauty

I, an observer, and poet in my own right,
Happened upon many strange characters on my journey's sights
Some happy, some sad, strong and some meek.
Ans on occasion, pursed lips soft-spoken tongue in cheek.
No matter how foreign a man was to me, I was the alien among them
Spoken language inconsequential, it was their hearts I yearned to learn

Between the tattered wings and broken halo
Fleeting a sadder note played on a villain and cello
I find myself walking
Running away from what I know is the truth:
I left Eden to chase a false sense of adventure

What the hell I was doing
I found myself choosing
My convictions led me to a foreign land
To give up everything that I knew,
Leaving behind a safe world to be made new

This journey makes us all grow in different ways
But nothing could make me stay the same
What a path life can pave!
No matter how steep or narrow, I stay the course

Though I miss my home and mountain view,
I yearn for adventure and travels turning me new
The road, sky, and sea stir a fresh feeling in me
The journey teaches a man to look beyond all that he can see

85

Dreams of Silhouettes

It was there I saw the light
Of all places it had to be there
The place of calm
The place of rest
My weathered body had traveled the beaten path
My feet could carry me no further

It was there at my most vulnerable when I saw in full vision
Shadows hide all imperfection, yes this is true
But the shadows cannot hide the soul
The soul takes its mighty form, no matter how big or small, loud or quiet
Beautiful-
Or ugly

She still dances
Whether in light or darkness, she remains the same
Her form strong and flexible like willow branch
Her movement elegant and pure like a swan gliding on water
With every fiber of her being she commits to the dance
I watched in admiration of the Silhouette Girl

Then she noticed me mid-step on my voyage
My heart froze as that glaze peered into my soul.
She was my judge for beauty
Words we never spoke
I felt my heart sink into the void
For my mind had furrowed her lips with heavy concern

But a soft touch of her palm on my check melted me

I, the loathsome man, the weathered man, did not deserve such kindness
Yet with no forethought she leaned in for that lovely kiss
With eyes shut I received her gift of acceptance and beauty
As the tears begun to fall; my eyes I opened
The golden morning hues warmed my face
She was gone
I sat up from my slumber in wonderment and awe

There is only one thing in this life that sums up all my regrets
I did not accept love, except in Dreams of Silhouettes

Thus ends our poems true
Told by a poet not old but new
The metaphor and hyperbole laid to rest
The mouth of modern lips did its best

Where hast thou thy poets been?
Arise O poet that lies within!
The heart that beats with passion bold
Tell thy tales before the grave robs you cold

About the Author

Abram Hollows was born and raised in Springfield, Missouri. During his life he has worked on his family farm in Colorado. At the age of 18 he enlisted in the US Navy. He was ordered to Naples, Italy where he had the pleasure of exploring Europe. During this time and a few years before, Abram began to write poetry. He has always been creative, working on many projects involving acting, and writing. Currently he still serves in the US Navy and continues to travel and work. He has served a total of 4 years and plans to continue to write under this pen name, Abram Hollows.

www.ingramcontent.com/pod-product-compliance
Lightning Source LLC
Chambersburg PA
CBHW031438130726
47989CB00003B/1192